Imagine the Sea

one hundred poems from a long walk

Tom Griffen

To Scotty, TR, and Big John

In 2018, Tom Griffen walked across the United States. His coast to coast journey is detailed in his book, *With a Good Heart: A Walk From LA to Brooklyn*. This poetry collection is its companion.

Contents

California

1

I'll just sit here
and wait for signs of life.
Touch my tongue to my wrists.
Imagine the sea.

2

Cross the bridge to where I'll stop.
Wave at passing cars below.
Frozen hands catch sunset fire.
Exxon light glows blue white cold.

3

The sand and grime
in joints and gears
creaks like old, slow bones.
My cart's wheels spin
and crunch gravel, dodge
death. My legs swing
wide strides over coyote parts.
Passersby twist necks
all the way around and
take their eye off the road
trying to read
the sign on my back.

4

5

It's not that I've forgotten you,
no—I just need something
to trigger my memory.

Arizona

6

Will I always have this itch to move.
Never have a comfortable chair
that smells like me, is shaped like me,
is marked by mustard stains and spilled beer.
I cannot say for sure.

7

You might tell me
you can see my tent
from your window.
But I know you can't.
You lie because
you are scared.

9

I sleep beneath
cotton sheets and
an extra blanket.
I can't get comfortable
and keep waking up
to rain and wind
scratching the tarp.
I dream of wild dogs
and human footsteps.
When I crawl
out of my bag
I squint at the sun,
peel a sweet tangerine,
and feel fog
seep into my skin.

10

The burner smells
like something's on fire.
All I'm trying to do
is boil water for tea.
I think it's splatter
from yesterday's soup
charring on red hot coils.

11

Falling rain, then hail
dampens the roar
from the mine.
Glass beads
scattering across
ceramic tile.
A broken bracelet.

13

Over the Gila River,
the winter sun bleeds orange.
Roosters crow. Goats
scratch their rumps
on a rusty car bumper and
when the see me,
they sound an alarm.
I imagine they are bleating
come get me, come get me.
I give chase and they scatter.

14

No matter what I think
there is no right way or wrong way.
Only the blowing hotel drapes.
And outside, a gliding hawk.

New Mexico

15

In tumbleweed nests
of brittle goathorns,
a family of quail presses
into a dusty corner. One calls
to warn of a forlorn tomorrow.

16

I sit alone
in the diner.
There's no hint
of yesterday's rain.
My silver dollar
pancakes are gone.
A ray of sun
warms my leg.
Nothing has changed.

18

Drivers peel into the lot
of a fast food drive-thru.
They shout their desires
into a box. It tells them to
please pull forward.
They do as instructed
and collect their bags
of food and cool drinks
and start eating before
leaving. Then they gun it,
chirping tires back into traffic.
This is loneliness.

19

A squawking animal
splashes in a flooded field.
The call resembles laughter
and I wonder if it, too, just recalled
the taste of its midday meal.
Chile verde chicken enchiladas.

Texas

20

The road is riddled with animal parts.
Corkscrewed bodies, sinewy wires.
I yearn for an orange.

21

Summer arrives unannounced
and turns the wind into a heater.

Not one car passes
the entire morning.
Pavement changes to dirt
and a van stops.
Three children and
their leather grandmother
offer me two dollars
for snacks at the market ahead.
They want to know if I am tired.

23

24

When I think of us
you are laughing.
When we talk on the phone,
I hear you frowning.

25

My hands reach for your skin
and touch nothing but my own.

26

A roadrunner stops, raises its tail,
then darts into a brush of sage.
It keeps an eye on me.

27

When I am close enough
to taste your salt, I will finally
stop staring at myself
naked in the hotel mirror.

29

I consider picking
purple and yellow flowers
from the roadside.
Tie the stems with dental floss
and mail them to you.
But I worry
you'll open the envelope
and the dry, crushed petals
will cover your lap and
you'll think I'm a fool.

The first rays of morning
brush my face
like a bull's eyelash might
brush a cow's cheek.

31

I find it so much easier to cry when it rains.

33

I move to the far edge of the shoulder,
lean on a tree and imagine her kneeling
on our blue plaid couch. She looks
out the window while birds visit the feeder:
the reckless male cardinal,
the patient Carolina wren,
and rarely, the red-breasted robins
who always come in a pair and take turns.

I wake up gasping,
choking on nothing.
Can a mouth, a tongue,
forget. Can hands.
My first thought this morning—
the bend of a woman's back.
Not yours.
The word it calls to mind—
yearning.

35

I make more plans:
Hike the Camino, the King's Trail,
the AT, PCT, the CDT.
Walk from Patagonia to Alaska
along the Pan American Highway.
Just walk and think and write.
These are all good things
but none include you.

Horses snort and chuff
as they race from the shade
to the fence line.
Their ripping muscles
cast small shadows.
They could easily
break through. But maybe
it never crossed their mind.

Arkansas

A wasp limps
across the hot sidewalk
heading towards tall grass.
It stops when
I stoop for a closer look.
Holds perfectly still.

38

When we were still in love,
our arms hooked tight
as we walked past
the place where we had
our first date.
The beers, the rickety stools,
the people coming and going.
I remember the sun turned to shade
and the evening became cool.
My longing makes no difference.

39

Leaves reflect sun.
My skin is red and hot.
There is no wind.

40

41

Sometimes our differences
in a shared memory
make me question everything.

42

I am unable to read her heart
and in this heat I no longer care
so I drink and drink and drink
and stay drenched with sweat
as the ocean gets closer.

43

She said she will not decide
if being together is a good idea.
She said she is too busy doing nothing
to think any more about falling leaves.

Mississippi

44

My aura is mosquitoes.
I sleep behind the rest stop
and dream of starting a new job.
I wake up worried I made
the wrong choice but
it's too late to go back and
change things because
everyone is counting on me and
I don't want to let anyone down.

45

I may have forgotten your name
but I can't shake how you made me feel.

46

Pull to the side of the road
for a short break. Water and jerky.
Take a deep breath and savor the
teriyaki on my tongue.
Is this umami. I don't really know
what that word means.
I pick a bit of dried meat from between
two molars. The space where food always
gets trapped. I'm going to need a filling.
I've had enough to know the signs.

47

I hold my breath
for one hundred steps and
listen to rice birds.
As I say ninety-nine out loud
I find a woman sitting alone
at a park bench
drawing circles
in a spiral notebook.
She tells me
I have to start over.

49

All that's been is here still.
That's a heck of a thought, isn't it.
All the shoes, the tires, the glass, the cans,
the wrappers, the cigarette butts, the love
letters, the belts, the saddles, the whips,
the machines, the posters, the art,
the peels, the bones, the gold teeth.
Nothing goes anywhere, really.
I sleep on a slope. Under a dead tree.

Alabama

50

All here is unfamiliar
so I think of songs from childhood
and sing words I never really knew.
Rhinestone Cowboy and
Pilot of the Airwaves and
Goodbye Yellow Brick Road.
What happened to that girl
who taught me to kiss with my tongue.
The one who told me she
accidentally sliced her wrists
jumping over a chain-linked fence.
She had a killer left hand
reverse layup. She taught me
what it feels like to lose.
I remember her lips
because they were blood red
and full. But for the life of me
I can't remember her name.

51

As the fog disappears
I realize the ocean
is not an ocean after all.
Because ocean is just a word
and saying a thing
doesn't make it real.
Yesterday, potato chips.
Salt and vinegar.
Today, melted Tillamook
and broken crackers.
A hawk. An airplane.
A picnic table. Green.
I believe this can happen.
I believe all of this is true.

53

54

I forget entire years.
Then something happens
to spark my memory
and for a couple weeks
I cry every time I see
a couple holding hands.

Tennessee

55

Ospreys circle over traffic.
Calling calls,
feeding chicks.
Carrying sticks
to thicken their nests.
Drivers see and hear nothing.

56

57

Beauty from afar.
Junk up close.
Junk from afar.
Beauty up close.

58

I am excited by
the mess in the road ahead.
When I reach it—
ten thousand crushed turtles.

59

I sit against the wall
of a gas station
to organize change
in my wallet.
Squint under
fluorescent lights
and see everything.
Someday all of this
will be gone.

60

61

I pick up a rusted car part.
I think it's a car part, anyhow.
It's definitely human-made
which means someone
spent time with it.
I rub my fingers along its
bumps and curves then
brush my thumb and index together.
The red dust is cinnamon.

Virginia

I whisper a secret
into the mouth
of a shot up mailbox.
It's cool and blue and
its metal flag is bent.
Afterwards, there's
a noticeable lightness
in my step.

63

I lay in bed at a cheap hotel.
Outside, the parked roar
of 18-wheelers.
I get up to pee, then toss and turn
and can't get back to sleep.

64

This view must change
before anything can happen.

65

I need to walk
seven more miles
to reach your hiding spot.
Seven is nothing.
There have been days
when I've done forty.
But my feet are heavy and
caked with mud and
wet concrete.
I know I'm sleeping. Still,
I'm afraid if I wake up
you'll be gone forever.

67

A hay bale far ahead.
I admire it, and liken the detail
of a painting.
A closer look—swarms of insects,
plastic bottles stuffed into grassy layers.
An empty cigarette pack.
Nearby, piles of human feces.

68

69

All those things we used to do—
all those things are now gone.
Memories stack atop memories
and whatever the truth actually is
doesn't matter. A small yellow bird
flies past, singing. It is real.

West Virginia

70

A little boy, dirty
around his mouth,
runs into the lawn
and waves like he's been waiting
for me to arrive. His mother
rushes out of the house,
screaming for him to
get his goddamned ass
inside right now.

71

Miss You spray painted
on the pavement.
No you don't, I say,
and keep on walking.

72

It's ok if empty spaces
are filled with ghosts.

Imagine the Sea

73

Maryland

74

Boys on the stoop
make jokes about my cart.
One asks what I'm doing
and they turn into statues.

75

Beer So Cold
it Hurts Your Teeth.
I want it and don't want it
at the same time.

77

A front yard sign says,
Self Serve Honey.
I want to add a comma.
There was a lady at a diner
who set my plate down gently.
Told me to take my time.
Told me she'd be
right over there
if I need her.

Pennsylvania

79

Around every curve,
the sound of chopping wood.

80

For a moment I hear the ghosts
of Civil War soldiers. Or maybe
it's the voices of children. Or
the wind. A mountain of Harleys
explodes over the foggy ridge.
I stop counting after sixty-one and
think about olive mushroom pizza.

81

For a few hours each morning
the thought of afternoon disappears.

83

In America
one of the ways
we celebrate culture
is by selling it.

84

Leaves, petals,
fast foot wrappers,
and sandwich scraps.
One pass with a broom
and everything changes.

New Jersey

The old man unveils
his time machine:
Next time you go
to a friend's house,
go a different way.

86

I thought maybe as I crested
the bridge and saw the ocean
I'd be overcome with awe.
Instead I stop for lunch at
a park bench, eat a can of beans and
a pouch of white tuna in water.
I forget all about the ocean
and wish I had
an extra Snickers bar.

88

Wake to the sound
of no sound.
Shadows from insects
dot the roof of my tent.

89

I take photos of butterflies
and try to capture things
I'd see better without this camera.

90

I fill a bag with trash
left by previous campers,
set up my tent
in a midday shady spot,
then eat watermelon and
do ecstasy with nudists.

91

Yesterday the ferry was cancelled.
Today I board and make eye contact
with a child who quickly hides
behind his mother's tan leg.

92

The rain stops.
An old woman
wearing a scarf
makes her way
to the top deck
and puts one hand
on her chest. She
grips the steel rail
as the city skyline
comes into view.

New York

93

94

A stranger
in Times Square
asks to have
her picture taken
with me.

I wonder what
being with
someone
actually means.

96

After stretching my legs
and eating a bowl of oatmeal,
I go outside and consider
whether or not I should
put on a sweatshirt.

97

The security guard at a museum
near Central Park says it's ok
to use the restroom.
There's softness in his eyes.
Or maybe it's longing.

98

The sound before the sight.
The smell before of the sound.
The idea before everything.
The impetus, the inspiration.
A cup of coffee with a friend.

99

I scream at the sea.
A man in saggy trunks
lifts his arms
and screams too.

100

There is no
right way.
There is only
the way
I am going.
Murmurations
and symmetry.
Just right, as is.

About the Author

TOM GRIFFEN was born in a California cowtown but spent his formative years along the Erie Canal in upstate New York. He earned his MFA in poetry from Pacific University in Forest Grove, Oregon. Tom is a freelance writer, visual artist, and a corporate trainer in the world of specialty run retail. He resides in Spokane, Washington on the third floor of an old printshop. In his spare time he carves wooden spoons and enjoys a well-crafted 6 oz. americano or a hazy IPA.

Find him on Facebook, follow him on Instagram @tomgriffen, and subscribe to his blog at tomgriffen.com.

Made in the USA
Monee, IL
02 December 2020